Maths Together

There's a lot more to maths than numbers and sums;
it's an important language which helps us describe, explore and
explain the world we live in. So the earlier children develop
an appreciation and understanding of maths, the better.

We use maths all the time – when we shop or travel from one
place to another, for example. Even when we fill the kettle we
are estimating and judging quantities. Many games and puzzles
involve maths. So too do stories and poems, often in an
imaginative and interesting way.

Maths Together is a collection of high-quality picture books designed to
introduce children, simply and enjoyably, to basic mathematical ideas –
from counting and measuring to pattern and probability.
By listening to the stories and rhymes, talking about them and asking
questions, children will gain the confidence to try out the mathematical
ideas for themselves – an important step in their numeracy development.

You don't have to be a mathematician to help your child
learn maths. Just as by reading aloud you play a vital role in their
literacy development, so by sharing the *Maths Together* books with
your child, you will play an important part in developing their
understanding of mathematics. To help you, each book has detailed
notes at the back, explaining the mathematical ideas that it
introduces, with suggestions for further related activities.

With *Maths Together*, you can count on doing the
very best for your child.

For Ann
Let me count the ways
R.W.

For my parents
C.J.

First published 1993 by
Walker Books Ltd
87 Vauxhall Walk
London SE11 5HJ

This edition published 1999
10 9 8 7 6 5 4 3 2 1

Text © 1993 Rick Walton
Illustrations © 1993 Cynthia Jabar
Introductory and concluding notes
© 1999 Jeannie Billington and Grace Cook

This book has been typeset in
ITC Officina Sans.

Printed in Singapore

British Library Cataloguing in Publication Da
A catalogue record for this book is
available from the British Library.

ISBN 0-7445-6828-5 (hb)
ISBN 0-7445-6802-1 (pb)

HOW MANY?

Rick Walton   Illustrated by Cynthia Jabar

WALKER BOOKS
AND SUBSIDIARIES
LONDON • BOSTON • SYDNEY

He is nimble. He is quick.
How many jump the candlestick?

One
Jack.

Spiders like to steal her seat.
How many things does Miss Muffet eat?

Two
Curds and whey.

Goldilocks sleeps all alone.
How many bears are coming home?

Three
The mama bear, the papa bear and the baby bear.

Snowy, cloudy, sunny, clear.
How many seasons in a year?

Four
Winter, spring, summer, autumn.

Pearl ring, gold ring, wedding band.
How many fingers on your hand?

Five
Little finger, ring finger, middle finger,
index finger, thumb.

See them hunting on the lawn.
How many legs do ants walk on?

Six

Left front, right front, left middle,
right middle, left back, right back.

Rainbows follow storms in March.
How many colours in the arch?

Seven
Red, orange, yellow, green, blue, indigo, violet.

Father Christmas flies away!
How many reindeer pull his sleigh?

Eight
Dasher, Dancer, Prancer, Vixen,
Comet, Cupid, Donner, Blitzen.

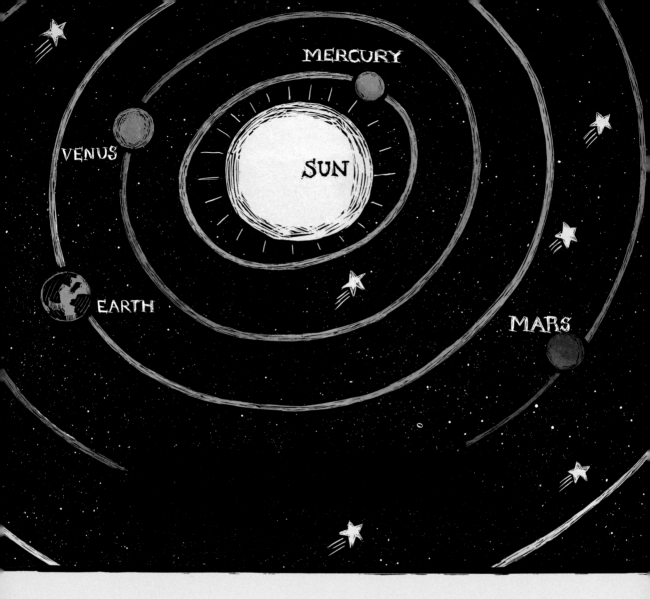

Round and round in space they run.
How many planets ring the sun?

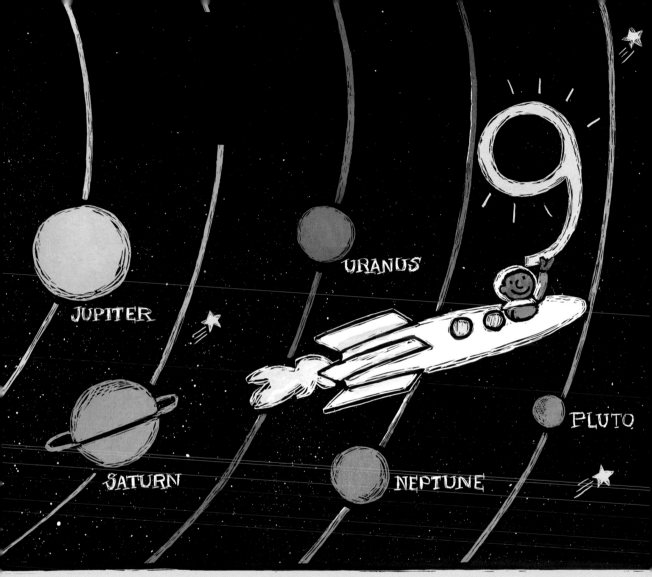

Nine
Mercury, Venus, Earth, Mars, Jupiter,
Saturn, Uranus, Neptune, Pluto.

Call me if you feel alone.
How many numbers on a phone?

Ten
Zero, one, two, three, four, five,
six, seven, eight, nine.

It's a goal! The players scream.
How many on a football team?

Eleven
Four defenders, four midfielders, two strikers
and a goalkeeper.

Holidays bring much good cheer.
How many months make up a year?

Twelve

January, February, March, April, May, June, July,
August, September, October, November, December.

About this book

How Many? introduces young children to several aspects of counting and number in an enjoyable way.

The numbers are shown in words, pictures and numerals. They appear in order from 1 to 12 through the book, so that children can practise counting in sequence. This is a good way for them to learn numbers.

How Many? also shows that objects can be counted in groups as well as one at a time. The eight reindeer are pictured in twos and the fingers are in fives. When children count the football players they find that 11 can be made up of 4, 4, 2 and 1. By showing that a big number can be broken down into smaller numbers the book introduces children to the ideas of adding and taking away.

Talking about the book together – the pictures, the numbers, and how they are grouped – gives you and your child the opportunity to use numerical language such as *how many altogether, more than, less than, not enough, lots, first, second* and *last.*

Notes for parents

There are lots of different opportunities for counting in *How Many?* You can point to each item as you count together.

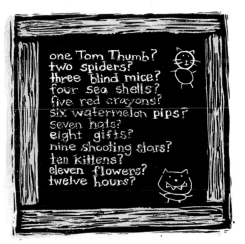

one Tom Thumb?
two spiders?
three blind mice?
four sea shells?
five red crayons?
six watermelon pips?
seven hats?
eight gifts?
nine shooting stars?
ten kittens?
eleven flowers?
twelve hours?

See if your child can find all these things in the book.

So how many didn't jump the candlestick?

You can use everyday activities to encourage your child to count with you, or by themselves.

I've scored three goals. What about you?

I've got four!

Children will see how to count and how useful it is when they watch you counting in different situations.

Hands up for orange juice. One, two, three...

It's not fair – Sophie's got more than me.

You can often help your child to work out a problem by asking questions rather than giving them the answers straight away.

How many more shall I give you then?

I've got five balloons.

Young children can easily make mistakes. Try not to say that they are wrong, but encourage them instead.

Good. Let's just count them again.

Children can learn a lot about numbers by playing board games with dice. They hear the numbers, see numerals, count the dots and move the same number of places along the board. They are also using number words as they play.

You can make a number line together by writing numerals on paper or card and hanging them on a piece of string. Use them to play games by muddling up the numbers, taking some away, or turning them round. You can play with fridge magnets, too.

Maths Together

The *Maths Together* programme is divided into two sets – yellow (age 3+) and green (age 5+). There are six books in each set, helping children learn maths through story, rhyme, games and puzzles.